Raccoons

Sarah Harvey

Explore other books at:
WWW.ENGAGEBOOKS.COM

VANCOUVER, B.C.

WWW.ENGAGEBOOKS.COM

Raccoons: Level Pre-1
Animals in the City
Harvey, Sarah 1950 –
Text © 2022 Engage Books
Design © 2022 Engage Books

Edited by: A.R. Roumanis

Text set in Epilogue

FIRST EDITION / FIRST PRINTING

LIBRARY AND ARCHIVES CANADA CATALOGUING IN PUBLICATION

Title: Raccoons / Sarah Harvey.
Names: Harvey, Sarah N., 1950- author.
Description: Series statement: Animals in the city
Engaging readers: level pre-1, beginner

Identifiers: Canadiana (print) 20220396345 | Canadiana (ebook) 20220396353
ISBN 978-1-77476-736-8 (hardcover)
ISBN 978-1-77476-737-5 (softcover)
ISBN 978-1-77476-738-2 (epub)
ISBN 978-1-77476-739-9 (pdf)

Subjects:
LCSH: Readers (Elementary)
LCSH: Readers—Raccoon.
LCGFT: Readers (Publications)

Classification: LCC PE1119.2 .H37 2022 | DDC J428.6/2—DC23

This project has been made possible in part by the Government of Canada.

Canada

Raccoons are very cute!

Raccoons love living in cities.

Raccoons have black-and-white masks.

Masks

Their tails have rings.

Tails

Raccoons have five toes on each foot.

Toes

Raccoons can unlock doors and open garbage cans.

11

They can hear a worm underground!

Worm

13

Raccoons sleep during the day.

They prowl at night.

Raccoons are strong swimmers. They do not like it very much.

They can run quite fast when they need to.

19

In cities, raccoons make dens in trees, attics or even chimneys.

Baby raccoons
are called kits.

In the winter, raccoons sleep a lot in their dens.

25

Raccoons will eat almost anything, even garbage. Keep your trash cans locked!

Raccoons are wild animals. It is not safe to touch or feed them. If you see one, give it some space.

Thank you for leaving me alone!

Explore other books in the Animals In The City series.

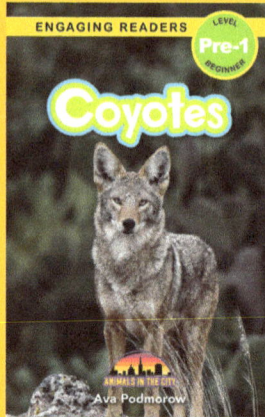

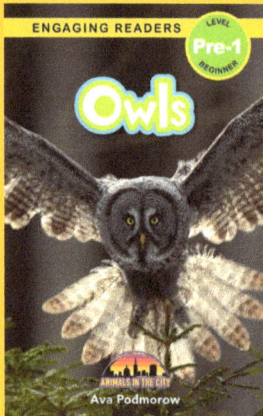

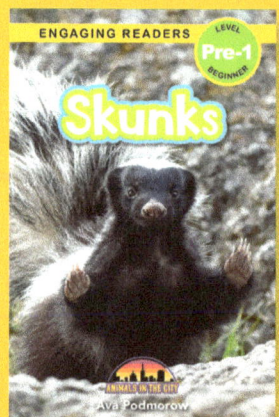

ENGAGING READERS — LEVEL Pre-1 BEGINNER
Cats
ANIMALS IN THE CITY
Ava Podmorow

ENGAGING READERS — LEVEL Pre-1 BEGINNER
Coyotes
ANIMALS IN THE CITY
Ava Podmorow

ENGAGING READERS — LEVEL Pre-1 BEGINNER
Deer
ANIMALS IN THE CITY
Ava Podmorow

ENGAGING READERS — LEVEL Pre-1 BEGINNER
Owls
ANIMALS IN THE CITY
Ava Podmorow

ENGAGING READERS — LEVEL Pre-1 BEGINNER
Pigeons
ANIMALS IN THE CITY
Ava Podmorow

ENGAGING READERS — LEVEL Pre-1 BEGINNER
Rabbits
ANIMALS IN THE CITY
Ava Podmorow

ENGAGING READERS — LEVEL Pre-1 BEGINNER
Raccoons
ANIMALS IN THE CITY
Sarah Harvey

ENGAGING READERS — LEVEL Pre-1 BEGINNER
Rats
ANIMALS IN THE CITY
Ava Podmorow

ENGAGING READERS — LEVEL Pre-1 BEGINNER
Skunks
ANIMALS IN THE CITY
Ava Podmorow

Visit www.engagebooks.com/readers

Explore level 1 readers with the Animals That Make a Difference series.

ENGAGING READERS — LEVEL 1 — Bees — ANIMALS — Jared Siemens

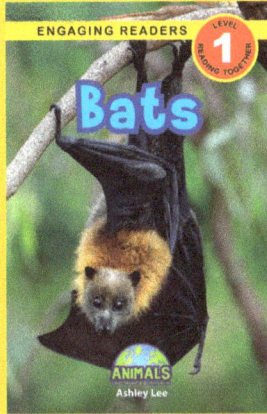
ENGAGING READERS — LEVEL 1 — Bats — ANIMALS — Ashley Lee

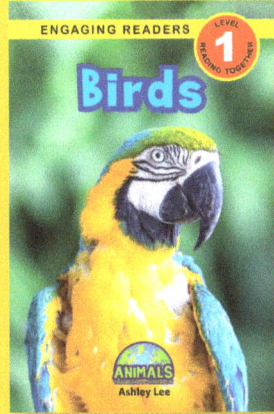
ENGAGING READERS — LEVEL 1 — Birds — ANIMALS — Ashley Lee

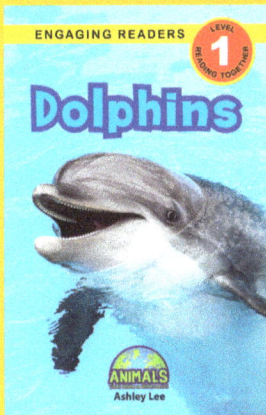
ENGAGING READERS — LEVEL 1 — Dolphins — ANIMALS — Ashley Lee

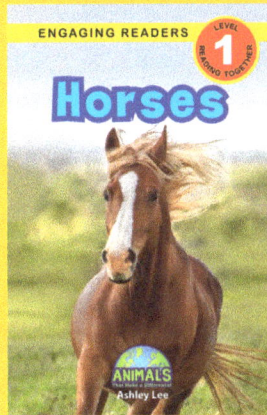
ENGAGING READERS — LEVEL 1 — Horses — ANIMALS — Ashley Lee

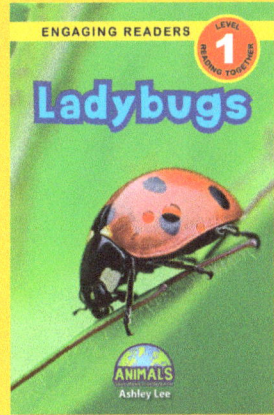
ENGAGING READERS — LEVEL 1 — Ladybugs — ANIMALS — Ashley Lee

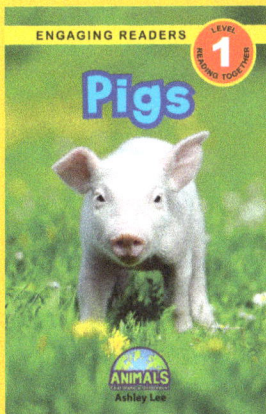
ENGAGING READERS — LEVEL 1 — Pigs — ANIMALS — Ashley Lee

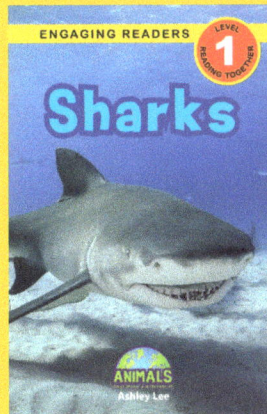
ENGAGING READERS — LEVEL 1 — Sharks — ANIMALS — Ashley Lee

ENGAGING READERS — LEVEL 1 — Squirrels — ANIMALS — Ashley Lee

Visit www.engagebooks.com/readers